# COLLEGE
# FOOTBALL

DiscoverRoo
An Imprint of Pop!
popbooksonline.com

Robert Cooper

abdobooks.com

Published by Pop!, a division of ABDO, PO Box 398166, Minneapolis, Minnesota 55439. Copyright © 2020 by POP, LLC. International copyrights reserved in all countries. No part of this book may be reproduced in any form without written permission from the publisher. Pop!™ is a trademark and logo of POP, LLC.

Printed in the United States of America, North Mankato, Minnesota.

052019
092019

THIS BOOK CONTAINS
RECYCLED MATERIALS

Cover Photo: John Mersits/Cal Sports Media/Zuma Wire/ AP Images

Interior Photos: John Mersits/Cal Sports Media/Zuma Wire/ AP Images, 1; Gregory Fisher/Icon Sportswire/AP Images, 5; Shutterstock Images, 6, 7, 15, 31; Red Line Editorial, 8, 22–23; Aaron M. Sprecher/AP Images, 9, 30; Todd J. Van Emst/AP Images, 11 (top); iStockphoto, 11 (bottom), 12, 14; Rob Carr/ AP Images, 13; John Fisher/Cal Sport Media/Zuma Wire/AP Images, 17; Douglas Stringer/Icon Sportswire/AP Images, 18;

Butch Dill/AP Images, 19; Nick Wagner/Austin American-Statesman/AP Images, 20–21; Peter B Joneleit/Cal Sport Media/Zuma Wire/AP Images, 25; Mike Stewart/AP Images, 26; Ross D. Franklin/AP Images, 27; David J. Phillip/AP Images, 28–29

Editor: Nick Rebman
Series Designer: Jake Nordby

Library of Congress Control Number: 2018964841

Publisher's Cataloging-in-Publication Data

Names: Cooper, Robert, author.
Title: College football / by Robert Cooper.
Description: Minneapolis, Minnesota : Pop!, 2020 | Series: Football in America | Includes online resources and index.
Identifiers: ISBN 9781532163739 (lib. bdg.) | ISBN 9781644940464 (pbk.) | ISBN 9781532165177 (ebook)
Subjects: LCSH: Football--Juvenile literature. | American football--Juvenile literature. | College football players--Juvenile literature. | College athletes--Juvenile literature.
Classification: DDC 796.33263--dc23

# WELCOME TO
## DiscoverRoo!

Pop open this book and you'll find QR codes loaded

with information, so you can learn even more!

Scan this code* and others

like it while you read, or visit

the website below to make

this book pop!

## popbooksonline.com/college-football

*Scanning QR codes requires a web-enabled smart device with a QR code reader app and a camera.

# TABLE OF
# CONTENTS

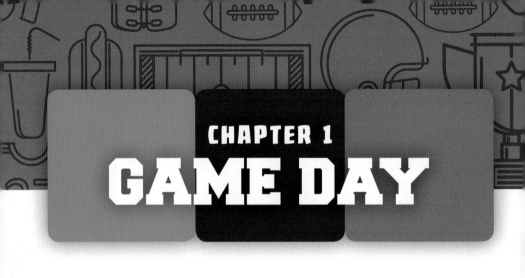

# CHAPTER 1
# GAME DAY

Fans fill the stadium. The lights are bright. Football players run onto the field. The fans cheer loudly. Then, the marching band plays the school song. It's time for a college football game!

WATCH A VIDEO HERE!

Penn State players take the field before a 2018 game.

*Alabama fans cheer on the Crimson Tide during a 2018 game.*

There are only 12 games in the regular season. That means each game is important. Fans support their team by wearing clothes with their school's logo and colors.

*Michigan Stadium is known as the Big House.*

The big crowds make college football games fun. Many stadiums can hold more than 50,000 people. A few stadiums hold more than 100,000 people.

**DID YOU KNOW?**

**Michigan Stadium can hold more than 107,000 people.**

# LARGEST STADIUMS IN COLLEGE FOOTBALL

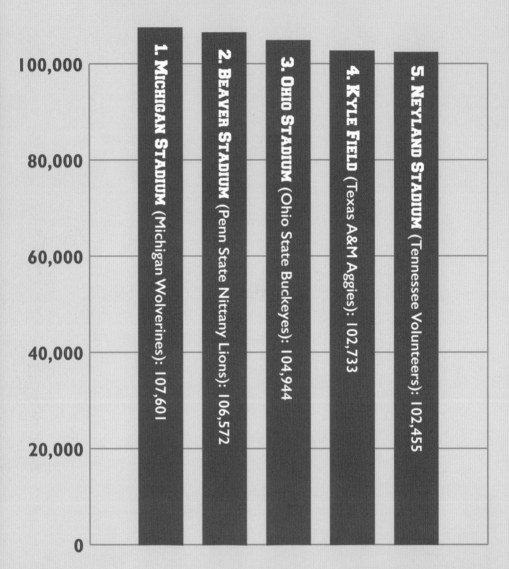

| | |
|---|---|
| 100,000 | |
| 80,000 | |
| 60,000 | |
| 40,000 | |
| 20,000 | |
| 0 | |

1. **MICHIGAN STADIUM** (Michigan Wolverines): 107,601

2. **BEAVER STADIUM** (Penn State Nittany Lions): 106,572

3. **OHIO STADIUM** (Ohio State Buckeyes): 104,944

4. **KYLE FIELD** (Texas A&M Aggies): 102,733

5. **NEYLAND STADIUM** (Tennessee Volunteers): 102,455

*Accurate as of 2019*

Every college has **traditions**. One tradition is the school's fight song. Many teams also have a mascot. The mascot is often a person in a funny costume. The mascot helps get the crowd excited.

*Sebastian the Ibis leads the Miami Hurricanes onto the field.*

# CHAPTER 2
# STUDENT ATHLETES

College football players are student athletes. They take classes like any other college student. But they also spend lots of time practicing. Most players at big colleges earn **scholarships**.

LEARN MORE HERE!

Auburn players take part in a summer practice.

*Studying is an important part of being a student athlete.*

Players must get good grades to stay on the team. Many players take their hardest classes in the summer. That way, they have more time to focus on football in the fall.

Myron Rolle was a star player at Florida State from 2005 to 2008. He also took difficult classes. Eventually, he became a doctor.

*Myron Rolle plays in a 2008 game against Maryland.*

## HOMECOMING

Most colleges have a homecoming weekend each year. It's a fun way to celebrate the school. Former students visit the college. They watch the football game. Many colleges also have parades, picnics, and other activities during homecoming weekend.

Student athletes are allowed to play for only four years. So, each team's **roster** changes every year. Some players graduate. New students come in and replace them.

*The Oklahoma marching band impresses the crowd at the homecoming parade.*

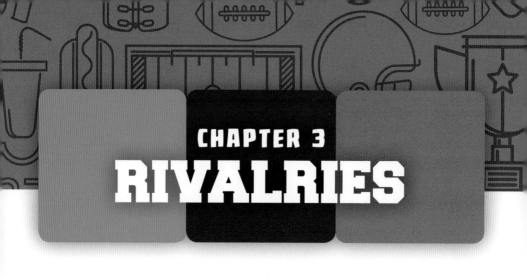

# CHAPTER 3
# RIVALRIES

Most college football teams have a **rival**.

Rivals usually play each other every

season. The fans and teams get excited

for rivalry games. Fans and players

believe it's extra important to beat

**COMPLETE AN ACTIVITY HERE!**

their rival. Some rivalries go back more

than 100 years.

*Wisconsin and Minnesota have
been playing each other since 1890.*

*Stanford and Cal are fierce rivals in the San Francisco Bay Area.*

Some teams are rivals because they are in the same **conference**. Each conference is made of several schools. Teams in neighboring states are often rivals. Sometimes, rivals are even in the same state.

Alabama and Auburn are in the same state. These schools have been rivals since 1893.

*Alabama receiver Henry Ruggs III catches a touchdown pass against Auburn in 2018.*

Many rivalry games happen on the

last weekend of the regular season.

Rivals often play for a trophy. For

example, Minnesota and Wisconsin play

*Texas players and fans celebrate after winning the Golden Hat in 2018.*

every year for Paul Bunyan's Axe. Texas

and Oklahoma play for a golden cowboy

hat. Illinois and Ohio State compete for a

wooden turtle.

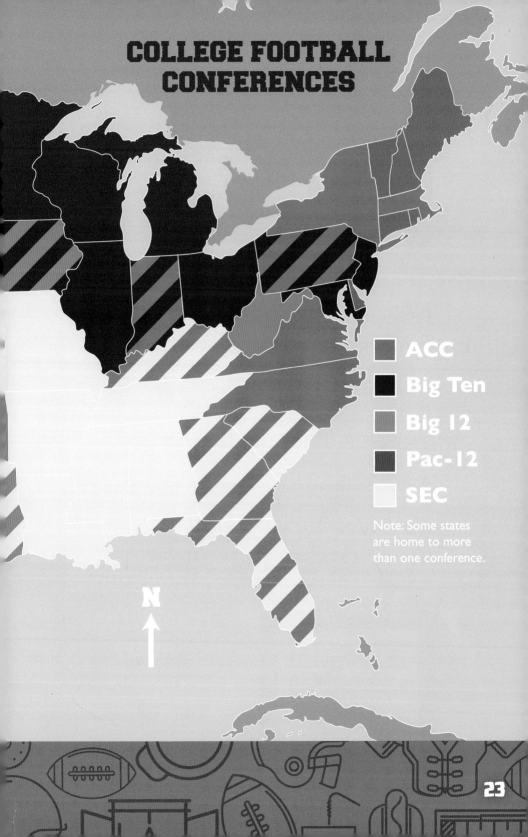

# COLLEGE FOOTBALL CONFERENCES

ACC
Big Ten
Big 12
Pac-12
SEC

Note: Some states are home to more than one conference.

N

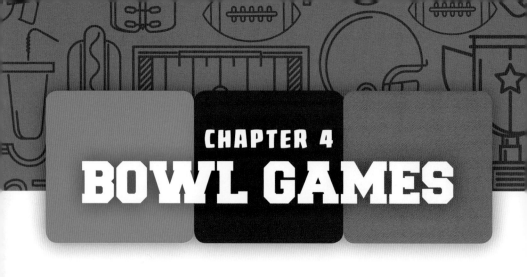

Bowl games make college football special. These games take place at the end of the season. Teams that have won six games or more are invited to play. Bowl games are a reward for a good season.

LEARN MORE HERE!

*Washington takes on Ohio State in the Rose Bowl after the 2018 season.*

These games are fun for both players

and fans.

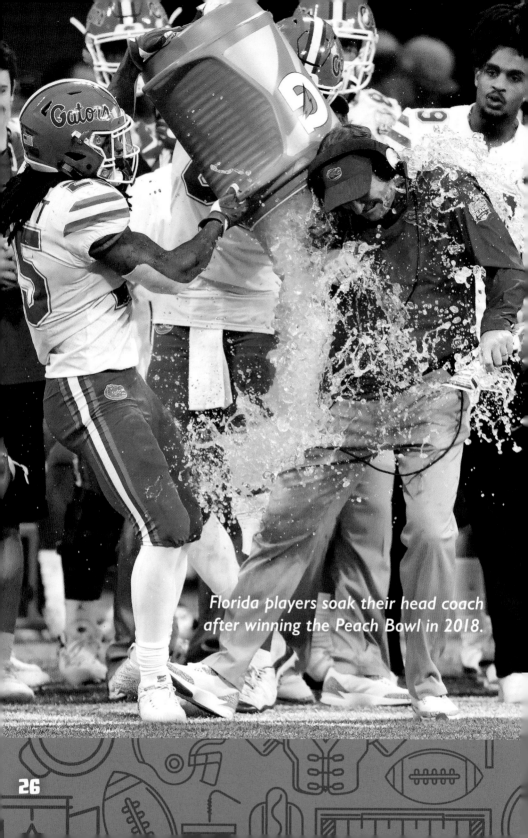

Florida players soak their head coach after winning the Peach Bowl in 2018.

*LSU receiver Justin Jefferson makes a great catch during the Fiesta Bowl in Phoenix, Arizona.*

Bowl games happen in December and January. These months are cold in the northern part of the United States. So, most bowl games are in warm places. They are often in states such as California, Florida, and Texas.

The four best teams in college football take part in the **playoffs**. The playoffs start with two different bowl games. The teams that win those games play each other for the championship. The winner of the championship is the best team in the country.

**DID YOU KNOW?**

In 2015, Ohio State won the first College Football Playoff National Championship.

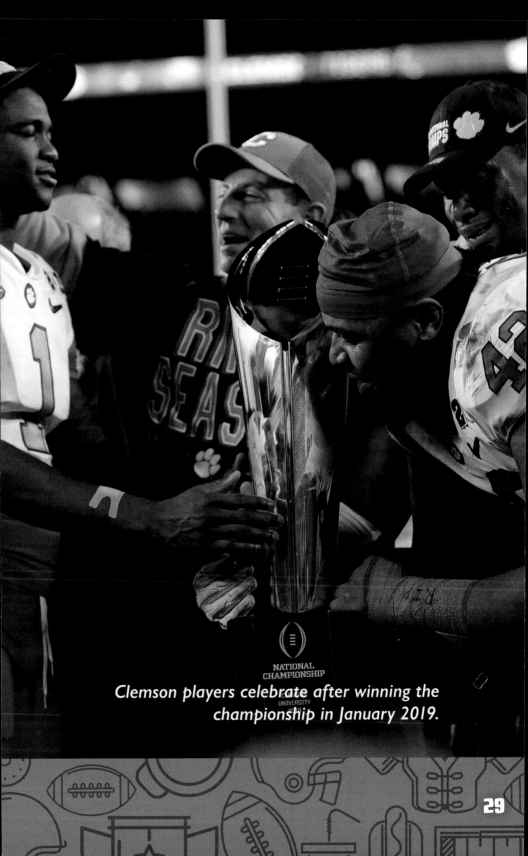

*Clemson players celebrate after winning the championship in January 2019.*

# MAKING CONNECTIONS

### TEXT-TO-SELF

Would you want to be a college football player? Why or why not?

### TEXT-TO-TEXT

How is college football different from other sports you've read about?

### TEXT-TO-WORLD

Thousands of fans go to college football games. Why do you think the sport is so popular with fans?

# GLOSSARY

**conference** – a group of teams that play one another every year and are in the same part of the country.

**playoffs** – the games at the end of the season to decide the championship.

**rival** – a team that has an intense, ongoing competition with another team.

**roster** – the list of players that make up a team.

**scholarship** – money an athlete receives to pay for school.

**tradition** – something people do every game to celebrate a team.

# INDEX

# ONLINE RESOURCES

# popbooksonline.com

Scan this code* and others like it while you read, or visit the website below to make this book pop!

## popbooksonline.com/college-football

*Scanning QR codes requires a web-enabled smart device with a QR code reader app and a camera.